All Scripture references taken from the KJV of the Holy Bible, unless otherwise indicated

When the Devourer Is Rebuked

by Dr. Marlene Miles

Freshwater Press 2022

freshwaterpress9@gmail.com

ISBN: 978-1-963164-08-4

Paperback Version

First Printing 2000, Second Printing 2002, Third Printing 2022

Table of Contents

WHEN THE DEVOURER

IS REBUKED

Freshwater

PREFACE

Accursed means, set aside for God's use. Jesus was set aside for God's use and God's purpose.

Christ hath redeemed us from the curse of the law, being made a curse for us; for it is written, Cursed is every one that hangeth on a tree, (Galatians 3:13)

Accursed is not the same as cursing (swearing), which is speaking profane words.

Out of the same mouth proceedeth blessing and cursing my brethren, these things ought not so to be, (James 3:10).

Nor is it the same as speaking negative things over people, as in cursing them.

> And Noah awoke from his wine, ... And he said, Cursed be Canaan; a servant of servants shall be unto his brethren,
> (Genesis 9:24-25)

and

> However, if you do not obey the LORD your God and do not carefully follow all his commands and decrees I am giving you today, all these curses will come upon you and overtake you, (Deuteronomy 28:16).

Some things that are **accursed** unto God are Jesus, and other people, certain cities, the tithe, and some offerings. Being accursed for God is a good thing, if you're obedient, and as long as what is *accursed* is brought into obedience.

INTRODUCTION

This might be a good time to check the pew you're sitting in for seat belts. Some of you might want to buckle up, secure yourselves in so you don't miss any of this word. Others may want to make sure you're free and unrestricted so you can leave quickly, once you hear what the Lord has to say today.

When it comes to money and *stuff*, we can be very short-sighted, selfish, narrow-minded, now-minded, and flesh-minded. We want money and the things that it provides, but many don't obey the laws by which money is provided to us. One Spiritual Law of Money is that if you tithe, God will rebuke the Devourer, (Malachi 3:10).

Tithing is paying one tenth of your increase to God every time you get paid, receive bonuses, commissions, or any increase. Tithing is not paying a large sum of money every now and then; it is paying 10% to God, regularly.

Today we will explore and put two subjects together in a new way: *tithing and living*. When you are through with this book, you will have a whole new appreciation for the Mercy of God. In this new appreciation you may also see some things that you've been wanting your kids to understand, such as how much you love them and want to help them. And that you really do want the best for them, no matter what they think, at times. Sometimes there is nothing you can do that your kids think is favorable.

Sometimes there are painful things that you must do in order to help them--, even though those things may be inconvenient or uncomfortable to them, for a season.

Yet, you continually pray that one day they will *get it*.

God is desiring that His children will *get it* too. Maybe when you *get it,* your children will also. Pray that this is **your** day.

THE ACCURSED THING

But the children of Israel committed a trespass in the accursed thing: …Achan, … took of the accursed thing: and the anger of the LORD was kindled against the children of Israel, (Joshua 7:1).

And Achan answered Joshua, … Indeed I have sinned against the LORD God of Israel, … When I saw among the spoils a goodly Babylonish garment, and two hundred shekels of silver, and a wedge of gold of fifty shekels weight, then I coveted them, and took them; and, behold they are hid in the Earth in the midst of my tent, and the silver under it, (Joshua 7:20-21).

Achan stole from among the spoils of Ai that God had called accursed. Accursed *means set aside for God's use.* Achan stole part of the tithe. The spoils from Ai were the **tithe** for Jericho.

The accursed stuff was found hidden in Achan's tent, and even though he confessed, by law, the people had to stone Achan to death. If that weren't enough, then they burned him with fire after they had stoned him. Is this the judgment of thieves, liars, and tithe-stealers? It was in the Old Testament, symbolic of eternal judgments, to suffer the first death and then suffer hell's fire.

But later in the Old Testament God says He will rebuke the Devourer for our sakes if we pay our tithes.

What does that mean? A rebuke is a strong scolding, a *calling back*. God will call the Devourer away from you when you are faithful to pay the tithe. God will repress or *check* the Devourer for you.

Having the Devourer rebuked really sounds good, doesn't it? But do we really want the Devourer rebuked? We say we do, but are we *really* ready? Are we disciplined, holy, obedient, and trustworthy enough to *tithe* so that God *can* rebuke him?

If the Devourer were lurking at your door, the only way He would have no right to enter your home is if there is nothing *accursed* in there. So, if there is nothing of God's in your house, that shouldn't be there, then you can answer, "*Yes*," to the rebuke-the-Devourer question.

But--, read on to see why I asked that in the first place.

Since God has promised to rebuke the Devourer, let's see how life would be in that ideal scenario.

Ananias and Sapphira (Acts 2) belonged to **The Church of One Accord** (or something like that). Anointing had been released corporately; the Holy Spirit of God was in full force. The people had all things in common. The Devourer was rebuked, and all was right with the world--, so it seemed.

Ananias and Sapphira came to church one day and *appeared* to tithe. They didn't even come empty-handed as many brazen souls do. They had what *looked* like a tithe in their hand, but they had held back part of the tithe. Since God cannot be mocked, and the Devourer was rebuked--, they died. They simply dropped dead.

Only model saints can be part of a model church and **LIVE**. Perfected (mature) saints who are obedient and disciplined are what I call model saints. So, the next time you start bellyaching and murmuring about your church, its imperfections, the leadership, the pastor, and et cetera; you'd better *think*! The imperfections in the church and in the other saints is why God is giving you Grace individually, and the church Corporate Grace, until you *get it together*.

Don't make the mistake of judging others while thinking you, yourself are ready to be judged, because you're not. Be patient and longsuffering because of spots, blemishes and wrinkles on your church, and the people in your church. Why? Because those imperfections are what's buying you time to get your house in order.

So why did what happened in **The Church of One Accord**, happen?

When you have God's stuff, He has the prerogative to **not stop** the Devourer from coming in to get it.

Why? Because He's mean?

No.

Because He's on a power trip?

No. It's because of Mercy. It is so God doesn't have to kill you!

Do I need to repeat that?

God allows the Devourer to come in and get the *Accursed* things, so God won't have to kill you!

The next time you start crying out to God to rebuke the Devourer, carefully consider if you are in right standing with God. You may be in order, but if God rebukes the Devourer and there are non-tithers present (in your home or church), they may suffer as Ananias and Sapphira, or as Achan and his family.

When you look at your tithing situation, you may be okay; but what about your sister, brother, mother, or your father? What's in their tents (houses)? The bones and the stones of Achan's **entire family** is also in the valley of Achor to this very day, (Joshua 7:24-26).

Don't be selfish trying to hurry up judgment. Instead, consider fully how your actions will affect your whole family, (your natural and church family.) But that doesn't mean don't tithe just because everyone else isn't.

THE TITHE IS PAID; THE OFFERING IS GIVEN

Another Spiritual Law of Money is: The tithe is **paid**, and the offering is *given*. The tithe is not optional, but the offering is at your discretion and choice; it is *given*.

I propose that if Abraham had not have tithed to a tenth of all to Melchizedek, (Hebrews 7:30), **Isaac would have been the tithe**. The tithe is paid, but the offering is *given*. Abraham paid tithes, therefore, making his offering optional (in a sense). God does not substitute the tithe, but offerings are free will and can be whatever you deem to give to God. If Abraham had not tithed when he was supposed to, Isaac would not have been substituted, instead, he would have been sacrificed. Just like you, after tithing, Abraham could give whatever he wanted to give in the offering, and not worry about having anything **taken** from him.

More on this in the book series: **Don't Refuse Me Lord: Why Is God Refusing My Requests?** by this author.

I am not saying that the Devourer is an agent of God, but God is still in complete control and has authority over him. And, so do you, in a sense. When you tithe, you keep the Devourer at bay. When you don't tithe, you break Spiritual Laws, and open the door for the Devourer and his greed. And he is very greedy.

THE DEVOURER

Who is this Devourer and what is he like?

The Devourer knows no bounds. He wants to still your praise and steal your worship. So, the first things he comes for is that which is set aside for God. He goes for what God wants. He goes for those things that are (or should be) God's. He goes for the tithe first, then the offering. The Devourer does this, so even if you have a fit of conscience later, you have nothing to offer God. You have no way to honor, serve, or worship the Lord. That's why so many new or undisciplined Christians lack physically as well as spiritually--, they may have finally come to the place where they really want to serve God, to tithe and give offerings, but they have used up, or lost all of their resources for doing so.

The Devourer has no limits and only stops when you stop him by your repentance, the Word and obedience; or God, again shows you **more Mercy**.

More Mercy means that God, who in Mercy allowed the Devourer, will stop the hand and the mouth of the Devourer *after he's consumed the* *accursed things*, to keep him from **completely destroying your resources for living, and *you* along with it**. This is to give you <u>time</u> to repent and get in step, or back in step with God.

WHAT DOES THE DEVOURER WANT?

The Devourer comes for the *accursed* things. If you've spent the tithe money, what you bought is also accursed. For example, if you spent the tithe money on your wardrobe, your closet door has just been opened for the Greedy One. You'll find that the Devourer attacks just that. Your clothes wear out fast, buttons drop off, things don't launder or even dry clean well.

Your clothes get shiny the first time you iron them, or you get those little balls on your favorite sweaters.

Your body doesn't cooperate, refusing to fit in even well-tailored and expensive clothes. Your good shoes hurt your feet; they get scratched, scuffed, or broken easily. The Devourer is ruthless, and he doesn't just stop at the *tithe* shoes. By your disobedience, he has gained access to the entire **Shoe Department** *of your closet*. That's why your shoes don't wear well, or why they wear out so quickly.

You might as well take a big, indelible marker and write on your clothes or shoes:

TITHE

(Lord knows! Don't get a perm with God's tithe money!) Many of you have already tried that, and when disaster followed, you blamed it on the stylist. The stylist was just as shocked as you; she'd never had that to happen before (except with other non-tithers). It wasn't operator error; it was that free-roaming Devourer that got in your hair and messed it up! And, since you don't go to that stylist anymore, she's happier than you are. You are walking trouble, with your non-tithing self.

Maybe you spent your money on your pride and joy: your car. That's why it doesn't work half the time. That's why it doesn't look good or run well. That's why you're always having trouble with it. Isn't it amazing that even though you've still got 43 payments left, what's wrong with it is never under warranty! The Devourer is ravenous, so he's not going to be satisfied with just inconveniencing you or costing you money. He won't stop until he completely destroys that car or costs you so much money that you no longer can afford the car (unless you put God in the position to rebuke him). The Devourer won't stop until your car is destroyed, repossessed, or totaled; that's his job. (Please don't offer me a ride in your accursed car.) You spent God's money on it--, it is God's car, and it is accursed, that's why the Devourer was able to put his hands on it. That's why it's not serving you. If you used any money that belonged to God for that car, it's accursed. And, God has a right to get His due. You might as well paint (or key) these letters on the side of your car:

GOD'S TITHE

You may find the same is true of washers, dryers, and refrigerators. Don't spend God's tithe money on personal or household stuff. If you want good grades, don't spend that tithe money on college tuition.

YOUR BODY

Most of the spiritual money talk we hear is in reference to the eating of seed. But it is possible to eat your tithe. Actually, if you are consuming what should be ministered to God, your tithe is the first thing you eat because the tithe comes *before* the offering (which is the seed). So, if you've eaten your seed, that was dessert; you ate (consumed, used up) your tithe first, as the appetizer and the main dish.

If you have eaten your tithe, you may have cursed your health. You might as well mark yourself, like Cain--, so nobody else will want to murder you, because God wants His tithe, (and so does the Devourer). Is God's tithe *in* you? Have you eaten it? You think God doesn't know?

You can't even hide drugs in your body, and not be detected by dogs or drug tests. Man has instruments so sensitive that they can measure the very lowest blood alcohol levels. Don't you know God is wiser than any man? God knows where you hid or tried to hide His tithe--, even if it's *in* you, (Psalm 139).

Seniors, especially--, repent! Maybe you didn't know any better, maybe you were just plain disobedient. Repent of robbing God all these years and live! That's not just old age you're suffering with, that could be the repercussion of years and decades of disobedience and robbery. While you're pleading with God for your health, healing, and your deliverance, repent of having robbed Him the past 20, 30, or even 50 years, and come, (or come back) into right relationship with Him.

Is that why so many are dead and dying: have they been robbing God?

Many have been robbing God for so long that it's simply a way of life. They've completely forgotten that they were supposed to tithe. Even sitting on church pews every Sunday, 80% of professed Christians don't tithe. Eighty percent of "God's people" are living with the Devourer, and in essence worshipping the Devourer. It's Friday, are you on your way to the mall instead of preparing your tithe? What gifts will you bring home to the Devourer this payday?

Not paying the tithe is sin, and sin is worship to some idol *god* or demon. Sin is the worship. When it is about money, then it is worship to Mammon.

No man can serve two masters: for either he will hate the one, and love the other; or else he will hold to the one, and despise the other. Ye cannot serve God and mammon, (Matthew 6:24)

Paying the tithe proves that we do not have Mammon sitting on the throne of our hearts.

HOW CAN I STOP THIS MADNESS?

God, moving in Mercy and Grace gave us the answer to the above question before He even revealed the problem. Read and heed:

Even from the days of your fathers ye are gone away from mine ordinances and have not kept them. Return unto me, and I will return unto you, saith the LORD of hosts. But ye said, Wherein shall we return? (Malachi 3:7, *emphasis added, mine.*)

He says that if we confess our sins, He is faithful and just to forgive us and cleanse us from all unrighteousness. Repent and return unto God in your tithes and offerings, and He will return unto you.

> If we confess our sins, He is faithful and just to forgive us our sins, and to cleanse us from all unrighteousness. If we say that we have not sinned, we make him a liar, and His Word is not in us (1 John 1;9-10).

Going forward, God visits to the 3rd and 4th generations; and, looking down your bloodline, you have obligation and authority to repent for your ancestors, as well. You have to repent for their having robbed God in tithes and offerings (if you know whether they did it or not--, just do it.)

Since God transcends all space and time, He will hear your prayers and declarations of repentance. He will honor your renouncements of rebellion, greed, and avarice through your family bloodline, and restore you to right relationship.

Make no mistake, the Devourer is not your friend. As you cry out to God, and He rebukes the Devourer from your life, you've certainly got to live right, or God will pass judgement on you, Himself. This is nothing to play with. This is real, and it is real life.

> … and that cannot cease from sin;
> beguiling unstable souls: an heart they
> have exercised with covetous practices;
> cursed children: (2 Peter 2:14).

Even in disobedience, God shows Mercy by allowing the Devourer to remove what is accursed from your camp, your house, and life so you can LIVE, hopefully in repentance and purpose, before it's too late.

YOUR CHILDREN

You love your children, don't you? They want Game Boys, toys, dolls, clothes, and cars. **Whatever you do, don't spend tithe money on your kids.** That will curse your kids, and that's not love.

Is that which is *accursed* in your kid's room? Are they handling it, touching it, using it, loving it? Here comes the Devourer, because you didn't take the tithe to the church; you spent it decorating your kids' room, or on their new clothes and toys. This is scarier than any horror film; the Devourer is in your house! The Greedy One may pass the door to your room, but there he goes, into your kid's room to get God's stuff. Think about what you're doing, people. By coveting God's tithe, you can curse your children, both generationally, and in the here and now.

Do you remember as a child your mother saying, *"If you don't clean your room, I'm going to do it for you?"* That should have sounded like a blessing, but it wasn't because you knew if your mom went into your room, you would not be able to find anything, ever again. It seems she would always throw away the most important stuff. By using the Devourer, this is one of the ways that God *parents* you.

Not to insult anybody's mom but the Devourer is kind of like that. The stuff you seem to treasure the most is the stuff that he comes for. As long as we keep acting like children concerning the tithe, God will parent us, by allowing the Devourer to come in and *clean* our rooms. The stuff that's in your house, that you treasured so much that you stole from God to get, is the stuff that opens the door for the Devourer, and it's what the Devourer comes to get *__first__*.

The Devourer comes for anything and everything--, **even your kids**. The Devourer is who (what) steals children, ruins them, destroys, or tries to destroy them. The Devourer's job is to turn the children away from their father, and their fathers away from the children.

Some of you can stop blaming or crediting God with your parental and material losses, it's you and the Devourer teaming up, tearing up and destroying things.

MARKED

If God rebukes the Devourer, what would you do? Rejoice, or lament?

When you see people walking or running to the altar to repent of having robbed God and recommitting to serving Him and becoming faithful in their tithes and offerings you should consider the gravity of the moment. You should pray to hear the seriousness of the altar call. If you are still robbing

God, you should run to repentance as fast as your Devourer-ridden body can take you. Not just because, but especially, as you see the last of your church's congregation coming into right tithing relationship with God. You don't want to be the last one. It's far too dangerous to be the last one.

Achan was the last one.

It's really a stupid risk being the last one. Ananias and Sapphira were the last ones to be obedient (the first ones disobedient).

In the Old Testament the people had a right to kill the non-tither, unless God marked them. Cain's gift was rejected, and he was **marked** by God, to save his life. Just like your stuff, if

God's tithe is in you, you are also *marked*:

ACCURSED

Like Cain, if God has marked you, it's to save your life, and buy you a little more time to get it together. If Cain had not been marked, man, God and the Devourer would have been on his trail. That's a losing battle; at least when man or the devil is after you, you can call on God--.

The Devourer comes in and conveniently, for your life and godliness, takes away the accursed things. But like the things you do for our own children, that they may not quite understand, Devourer work feels very uncomfortable and inconvenient to your flesh. But, if you are not a tither, every time the Devourer cleans you out, you should count it as Joy. God is giving you one more chance to repent and live right. And, God wants you to live in obedience instead of having to die; and to die in sin, heading for hell.

If you are a non-tither, is it because of greed? Without proper teaching and spiritual understanding, there is no way you or any of us will rejoice over financial material, physical and personal reversal. Things breaking, or constantly losing things and having to spend extra money all the time is exactly what nobody wants--, especially the greedy man. Even having to constantly spend money on doctors and medicine could be because of the Devourer being on duty. When financial setbacks occur, the non-tither will get angry and greedier, and may put off tithing even longer. That's just what the devil wants. See how the cycle continues, and works against people? This is bondage, and it puts people's prosperity, health, and lives in very dangerous standing.

DON'T BE THE LAST ONE

The purpose of this book is to educate, stimulate and challenge you to set you free!

If you are a tither, I cannot say that every time something breaks, or something bad happens that it's your fault. But have you considered the tithing history of your parents, grandparents, great-grandparents--, all your ancestors? God visits to the 3rd and 4th generations; perhaps you're paying interest and penalties on the money they robbed from God, years, and years ago.

You have authority and responsibility to **repent** for your ancestors.

When the Church was on One Accord, Ananias and Sapphira were the last ones to tithe--, but they did not actually tithe. In their church, the Devourer was rebuked, and that couple held back part of the tithe. God, who doesn't accept partial tithe payments, could not save them. God, who is full of Mercy and Grace could not save them. The Devourer was off the clock, he wasn't working that day, in that church, being that were on *one accord.* The Devourer can't come in when there is one accord (unity). The devil hates one accord because it puts him out of business. In that church, that day, the Devourer was rebuked; he was fired. So, there was no way to physically remove the accursed thing from Ananias and Sapphira's house, so they had to die.

God was not going to release the Devourer on an otherwise perfect church. He wouldn't do that to the entire Body, for just two sinners. He didn't do it for Ananias and Sapphira and they brought *something* to the church. How much less can God do for the people who don't bring *any* gift to church with which to honor or worship God.

Don't go to the church or be in a church where the Devourer is rebuked, if you don't tithe; that is a death wish. God cannot help you when you are stealing and hiding His stuff, and using it selfishly, no matter who you are in the church or what you do there. No church should allow you to bring them tithe trouble, as Achan brought to the camp!

Whoever you are, you can save, and improve your life with this decision: Decide to tithe; then do it.

Non-tithers, robbers of God, especially those who are lost and physically sick, the Devourer has damaged every part of your life that has touched, used, or communed with the *accursed* thing over the years, either slowly and subtly, or suddenly and in devastating ways.

You know.

And, unless you repent, return to God in your tithes and offerings, the Devourer continues his prowl, stealing, killing, and destroying.

The *accursed* things say, *"Come and get me!"* That's what lets the Devourer in.

RECAP

The tithe is paid; you owe it. The tithe is brought into your church; it is never split up.

The offering is given. Offerings may be and should be given to any place where you receive spiritual education either in person or by television, radio, or online. Do not tithe to a television evangelist or media church unless you don't have a local church.

If you don't have a local church and a good pastor, get one today!

Dear Reader

Thank you, dear reader for acquiring and reading this mini-book. May it make a difference in your life. May the tithe be placed in God's hands, and may He receive it as He received Abel's.

May your offerings bring a sweet-smelling aroma to the nostrils of God.

Until then, honor God every day of your life, and He will bless you, mightily.

Amen.

Dr. Marlene Miles

Other books by this author

(Highlighted books are of related subject.)

AK: The Adventures of the Agape Kid

AMONG SOME THIEVES

Ancestral Powers

Battlefield of Marriage (The)

Blindsided: *Has the Old Man Bewitched You?*

https://a.co/d/5O2fLLR

Churchzilla, The Wanna-Be, Supposed-to-be Bride of Christ

Demons Hate Questions

Devil Weapons: Unforgiveness, Bitterness,…

Dream Defilement

Don't Refuse Me, Lord (4 book series)
https://a.co/d/6tAqlaA

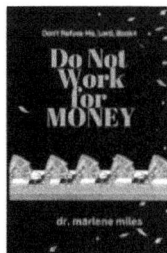

Every Evil Bird

Evil Touch

Fantasy Spirit Spouse

FAT Demons (The): *Breaking Demonic Curses*

The Fold (5 book series)
https://a.co/d/biwyxwa

The Fold (Book 1)

Name Your Seed (Book 2)

The Poor Attitudes of Money (3)

Do Not Orphan Your Seed (4)

For the Sake of the Gospel (5)

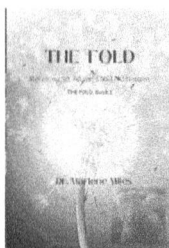

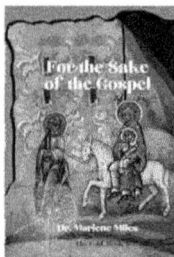

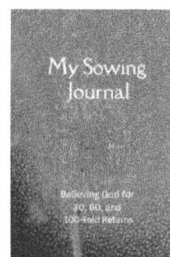

Gates of Thanksgiving

got HEALING? Verses for Life

got LOVE? Verses for Life

got HOPE? Verses for Life

got money? https://a.co/d/fwBJud3

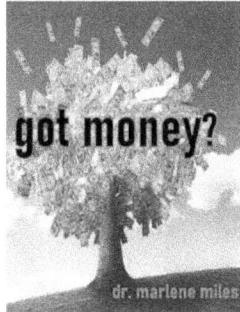

How to Dental Assist

How to Dental Assit2: Be Productive, Not Wasteful

Let Me Have A Dollar's Worth
https://a.co/d/jhFWpbF

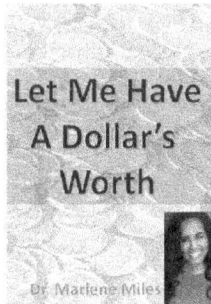

Living for the NOW of God

Lose My Location https://a.co/d/crD6mV9

Man Safari, *The* (mini book from Wilderness Romance)

Marriage Ed. Rules of Engagement & Marriage

Made Perfect in Love

Motherboard (The) ~ soul prosperity series

Plantation Souls

Power Money: Nine Times the Tithe
https://a.co/d/fjob745

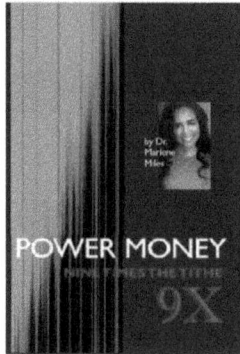

The Power of Wealth *(forthcoming)*

Rules of Engagement & Marriage

Seasons of Grief

Seasons of War

Sift You Like Wheat

Soul Prosperity soul prosperity series 3

https://a.co/d/5p8YvCN

Souls Captivity soul prosperity series 2

The Spirit of Poverty https://a.co/d/inFFfLY

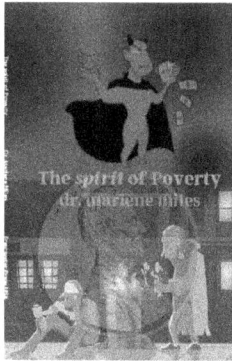

This Is NOT That: How to Keep Demons from Coming At You

Throne of Grace: Courtroom Prayer

Time Is of the Essence

Too Many Wives: *Why You Have Lady Problems*

Tormenting Spirits   https://a.co/d/dAogEJf

Triangular Power *(series)*

>   Powers Above

>   SUNBLOCK

>   Do Not Swear by the Moon

>   STARSTRUCK

Uncontested Doom

Upgrade: How to Get Out of Survival Mode

>   Toxic Souls (Book 2 of series)

Legacy (Book 3 of series)

Warfare Prayer Against Beauty Curses

Warfare Prayer Against Poverty

What Have You to Declare?

When the Devourer is Rebuked

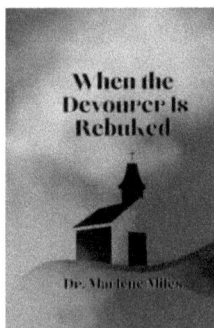

The Wilderness Romance *(series)*

- *The Social Wilderness*
- *The Sexual Wilderness*
  - *The Spiritual Wilderness*

www.ingramcontent.com/pod-product-compliance
Lightning Source LLC
Chambersburg PA
CBHW071734020426
42331CB00008B/2029